What Happened To Advertising? What Would Gossage Do?

What Happened To Advertising? What Would Gossage Do?

Massimo Moruzzi

What Happened To Advertising? What Would Gossage Do?

ISBN 978-8469727270

This book is dedicated to the memory of Paul Morales, Fabio Metitieri, Paolo Geymonat, Marco Zamperini and Alberto D'Ottavi. We miss you dearly.

Every profession bears the responsibility to understand the circumstances that enable its existence.

– Robert Gutman

Contents

Intro

Why is it all of a sudden so important that we "like" our favourite brand of butter on Facebook? Hype and bullshit are nothing new in the world of advertising, but things are getting out of hand.

Why don't people in advertising like their jobs anymore?

Interrupting people is fun, if you do it in a witty way, à la Bernbach; or nasty, if you punch people in the face, à la Rosser Reeves. In any case, it's their job.

Why do they want to do something else?

What is all this nonsense about "branding campaigns", "interactive advertising", or the suddenly so-important "conversations" between a brand of butter and consumers?

Isn't coming to terms with the fact that people on average don't like ads and have more important things to do in life other than hearing from companies the first, insufficient and yet necessary step to end the delusional thinking and start doing (creative) work that actually sells products?

In Chapter 1, we draw from my experience with web startups and try to understand what "branding" is and what it isn't, and why "branding campaigns" don't make any sense. We also ask: What happened to the Creative Revolution? Why has advertising slid from where it had worked so hard to raise itself [1] – from being a simple thing that is hard to do, i.e. using creativity to persuade people to buy something, to being an over-complicated and ridiculous "exercise in branding" that is apparently accessible only to the specialists who know the tricks of the trade and the jargon, but which doesn't solve the problem of creating demand for a product? Which players gain the most from this sad state of things? [2]

In Chapter 2, and later in Chapter 9, we take a hard look at what was once called "interactive advertising" and is now called "display advertising", i.e. advertising nobody "interacts" with. In spite of abysmal click-through rates, banner ads, largely dismissed after the Bubble, seem to be back in style. Should we rejoice? Does it make sense to spend money on banner ads? What has advertising on the web become, if not the reign of large-scale, low-quality direct response? Is this not a step backwards from the Creative Revolution, back to a system where the only things that count are media buying and scientific number crunching and creativity is at best a by-product? Are we wasting some of the best minds of our generation, at least amongst programmers and mathematicians, just to make online ads suck a little less? [3]

In Chapter 3, we take a step back in time and take a look at Howard Luck Gossage, a remarkable adman from San Francisco whose ideas and contrarian views about advertising seem as fresh today as they were back then. We concentrate our attention on a remarkable ad campaign Gossage did for Eagle Shirtmakers in 1961, and we ask: Why was Gossage more successful in his "interactive advertising" efforts half a century ago than anybody has ever been in the Digital Age? What can we learn from Gossage? How is it possible that *The New Yorker* in print half a century ago was much more of a "community" than either Facebook or Twitter will ever be?

In Chapters 4 to 8, we tackle the *nonsense du jour*, the current obsession with social media. We start by trying to disentangle all the babble about social networks, web2.0, user-generated content (UGC) and social media (Chapter 4); go on to challenge the conventional wisdom about consumers who, we are told, want to have "conversations with brands" (Chapter 5); question "The ROI of social media" (Chapter 6) and "The value of a Facebook Fan" (Chapter 7); and end up having to agree that the definition of social "media" made a lot of sense: Social networks have become nothing but private "enclosures" of the web where companies need to pay to promote themselves just like in any other type of media (Chapter 8).

Lastly, we go back to Gossage and try to guess what he would do were he around today. In Chapter 9, we try to make the case that Gossage would understand that advertising is not as important as it used to be, and that he would be happy about this. In Chapter 10, we speculate about what Gossage would do to take advantage of social media without falling prey to the hype and the bullshit of our era, and come to the conclusion that the sooner companies understand that the web is more of a lemon for them than it is an opportunity, the better.

Notes

1. "Doyle Dane Bernbach woke everybody up. The agency's string of stunning successes made a mighty persuasive argument for 'the new creativity'. As a result, more and more agencies come to the realization that the most important service they offered was not market research, or other support functions - it was the making of an ad". Dobrow, Lawrence, *When Advertising Tried Harder: The '60s: The Golden Age of American Advertising*, page 24.

2. Who gains the most? How about media companies and the huge advertising-marketing conglomerates?

3. "The best minds of my generation are thinking about how to make people click ads", says Jeff Hammerbacher. "That sucks". You can say Hammerbacher is a conscientious objector to the ad-based business model and marketing-driven culture that now permeates tech. *http://www.fastcompany.com/3008436/takeaway/why-data-god-jeffrey-hammerbacher-left-facebook-found-cloudera*

1

Branding

A long, long time ago, I worked for the only *dot.com* in the world without a dot. [1] Munich-based ciao|com did not have a dot because in German you say "ciao de" – and "ciao com", without pronouncing the dot. Hence, let's put in a "pipe" [2] instead of a dot in the logo. Brilliant idea.

On my second day on the job, the ad agency showed up to present the results from ciao|com's first extensive banner ad campaign. We were unhappy with the results. The creativity was asking people to sign up, and yet very few people were doing so. I was curious and a bit worried: Would I be smart enough to understand what had gone wrong and why?

Only a few minutes into the presentation, I found out that I needed not worry too much: They were trying to bullshit us.

All I had to do was refuse to buy it. "Your campaign was a hit on this website: The click-rate was 0.6%". "On this website it was lower, but your message was shown to the right audience". And when they had nothing good to show us at all, they told us it was: "Good for your branding". That's when I learned that stuff that doesn't work... that's code-named "branding".

Wait a second. Who told them that "clicks" were our goal? And how could they be so sure about which was the right audience for us exactly when the very first sign of interest, the click rate, had been even lower than in the other cases? Never allow other people to tell you which metrics you should be looking at. It's your budget and it's your responsibility. It's your job to figure out the infamous KPIs, or key performance indicators, you want to keep an eye on. Don't be distracted by the bullshit coming from people who are just after your marketing money. Lastly, why was this guy pretending to be an expert on "branding"? Who did he think he was, David Ogilvy?

I decided we would never again buy banner ads at CPM prices, or cost per thousand impressions. Cost per kilogram, as I loved to say, because the logic seemed to me to be as refined as the one by which you buy fruit and veggies at the market stall. We moved all our budget to any form of pay-per-click promotion we could find (this was a few years before Google AdWords), made sure it was as simple as possible to sign up to our website, gave visitors a good reason to do so and decided that people had to experience the bloody website for themselves. That's where we would make it or break it. That's where we were going to create a brand. Or not. Not with our ads. [3]

Next startup, French online dating company Meetic. While most of our business came from co-brands, i.e. from buying lots of "traffic" directly on web portals, we also tried banner ads with just one goal in mind: get clicks. [4] Get people to check out our website and hopefully sign up. Then prove to them that we were a better service than the other online dating websites that looked like places where you'd look not for romance but for a used car, and hopefully get them to pay. When I had to choose a PR agency for Italy, one of the people I was speaking with told me that our ads were "kind of low-quality" and that they were "ruining our image". "Oh, really?", I snapped back. I chose a different agency. [5]

Let's leave my *dot.com* years aside. Was it any different in the offline world, when we were dealing with cars and airlines, or toothpaste and shampoo? Not at all. Why should it have been any different? When and why did the absurd idea that you can create a brand just with ads – worse, with vague and empty "branding campaigns" [6] – come to pass? [7]

In the good ol' days, ads worked. Ads worked so well that everybody wanted to do ads. As things got crowded, both in terms of more ads everywhere all the time and in terms of an ever-higher number of different products and services sold on the market, ads started to work less well. It was not "magic" anymore. It was harder. Who was winning? Perhaps those who had the best products and who did the best ads? No, that would make it sound too simple. And so, probably true.

The answer many started giving was: "Those who have the best brand". But how did they get to the point that they had the best brand? They created the best ads, got the largest number of people to try their product or service, and as it was a great product... No, no, too simple once again. Those who had the best brand were those who did "branding campaigns"!

Who made up this bullshit, and why? Mediocre agencies found it simpler to babble about values, positioning, branding etc than to do the hard creative work [8] necessary to say something interesting enough about a product to help move it off the shelves. On the company side, it was a lot easier to think that the problem lied "with the brand", whatever that meant, than to work to improve the product, find the right price etc. Take care of the brand and "Everything's gonna be alright". Just like in that nice Bob Marley song. [9]

Agencies and their clients decided to settle for this fantasy world in which they had problems speaking with their kids, but somehow perfectly understood the finer details of the psychological profile of their "ideal target consumer" (instead of their real customers), and then went on to produce "branding campaigns" that would align them with these ideal consumers and bring them to totally and unconditionally love their brand. Or something along those lines.

But weren't some ads very important in the creation of a brand? Of course! But only precious few, which is exactly why we study those campaigns, be they the obnoxious repetition of the same message over and over again, as favoured by Rosser Reeves of Ted Bates (Anacin) [10], the classy and sophisticated copy of David Ogilvy (Hathaway Shirts, Schweppes, Rolls-Royce) [11], the self-effacing wit of Bill Bernbach (Levy's Bread,

Think Small, We Try Harder) [12] or the off-the-wall ideas of Howard Luck Gossage (Qantas, Pink Air, Eagle Shirtmakers). [13]

But no empty and vague feel-good, happy-shiny-people-holding-hands [14] "branding campaign" has ever created a brand. Nor has any banner ad campaign, to my knowledge. [15]

Notes

1. Being the only *dot.com* without a dot was remarkable, given that in those days even hardware companies and telcos went out of their way to be perceived as *dot.coms*. Here is ciao|com's *dot-less* logo.
   http://www.23hq.com/dotcoma/photo/20572123/original

   Sun Microsystems bragged that they were "the dot in dot.com".
   http://www.23hq.com/dotcoma/photo/20572129/original

   France Telecom started posing as France Tele.com. Très cool.
   http://www.23hq.com/dotcoma/photo/20572125/original

2. The "pipe" is also called Sheffer stroke, vertical line, vertical bar, verti-bar, vbar, stick, vertical slash etc.
   http://en.wikipedia.org/wiki/Vertical_bar

3. Nor were we going to create a brand with our custom-made proprietary company font for all our corporate communications. I kid you not. We had our own proprietary, custom-made font for all the oh, so very important corporate communications coming from a startup nobody had ever heard of. Ah, those were the times!

4. Our online advertising performed decently enough only when we were able to buy ads really on the cheap. No matter how aggressive we were with our in-your-face and click-baiting creativities, banner ad campaigns that performed well enough for us to invest in them on a steady basis were the exception, not the rule.

5. He was right, of course. But we did not care about "branding via advertising". It was way too expensive for a startup, and we didn't believe in it. All we were trying to do was to get people to sign up!

6. Who is to blame if Young&Rubicam call themselves a "BrandAsset Valuator"? Or if at Ogilvy they say they are "360 Degree Brand Stewards"? At Grey, apparently, they do "Brand Acceleration"; JWT is in "Brand Storytelling"; and even at DDB they now say that their job is "Positioning brands to compete", as noted in Parker, George, *The Ubiquitous Persuaders*, page 203.

7. George Lois says the culprits are Jack Trout and Al Ries and their seminal 1981 book *Positioning: The Battle for Your Mind*, in which they said: "Today, creativity is dead. The name of the game on Madison Avenue is positioning". Too bad that the idea of "slots" in consumers' heads is pseudo-scientific nonsense. Lois, George, *What's the Big Idea? How to Win With Outrageous Ideas (That Sell!)*, pages 33-42.

8. It's that creative spark that I'm so jealous of for our agency and that I'm so desperately fearful of losing. I don't want academicians. I don't want scientists. I don't want people who do the right things. I want people who do inspiring things. – Bill Bernbach's 1947 *Letter to Grey*, in Bernbach, Evelyn and Levenson, Bob, *Bill Bernbach's Book: A History of Advertising That Changed the History of Advertising*, page 112.

9. Bob Marley and the Wailers, *Three Little Birds*.

10. Was there not a nicer, kinder and smarter way to sell over-the-counter drugs? Of course there was. See (and read about) the pure brilliance of what George Lois did years later for Coldene. *http://www.georgelois.com/pages/milestones/mile.coldene.html*

11. Ogilvy, David, *Ogilvy on Advertising*, pages 10, 11, 14, 59, 79 and 87.

12. Cracknell, Andrew, *The Real Mad Men: The Renegades of Madison Avenue and the Golden Age of Advertising*, pages 26-30, 37-48, 64-68, 84-100, 125-131.

13. Harrison, Steve, *Changing the World is the Only Fit Work for a Grown Man*, pages 16-19 and 69-80.

14. That's another song: *Shiny Happy People*, from REM.

15. Especially not the ones nobody ever clicked on. Want to create a brand on the web? Get people to try out your service. Want to do it offline? Get them to buy your product. It's that simple.

2

―――

Interactive Advertising

When the web came along, different people would have liked it to become different things. For some it was "unconceivable that we should allow so great a possibility for service... to be drowned in advertising chatter". No, that's not Tim Berners-Lee. It's Herbert Hoover, then US Secretary of Commerce, talking about radio, in 1922. [1] But you get the idea.

Some people thought the web was going to enable top Universities to spread knowledge to the distant corners of the world. [2] Others thought it was the perfect place to sell dog food, hence the long series of "Amazon for pets" E-Commerce websites that were funded during the Bubble.

Advertising people, of course, thought it was going to be an advertising medium. Like TV, but better: "interactive".

The idea was that, for reasons which I have yet to understand, people would want to "interact" with ads. Thus the IAB, or *Interactive Advertising Bureau*, was born.

My first question is: Why in the world would you want anybody to "interact" with your ads? Wasn't the goal of advertising to convince people to buy your bloody product? Oh, right away – right from the ad, you mean? You must be day-dreaming. But, incredible as it may sound, many were.

This is exactly what many were hoping for: A consumer, one of those mythical creatures with two mouths and a credit card always ready in their hand, would see a product on a banner ad, click, get more information right in the banner ad and buy! Or, even better, they would see a product on TV, either in an ad or in a product placement during a show or a movie, interrupt whatever it was that they were watching, check out the product and buy it. Not going to happen. And it didn't.

How can people even come up with ideas like these? There's a lot of delusional thinking going on here, both on the part of marketing people and on the part of technology people.

Marketing people seem to think that everybody else's life centres on products and brands and goals and positioning and differentiation and so on just like their own lives do. Many people are indeed shallow, but luckily not that many people are that shallow. Marketing people seem to have trouble understanding that people have other goals in life and other things they derive pleasure from apart from shopping, and that they go online to escape ads as much as to find products.

One of the things marketers absolutely love to talk about is "engaged audiences". Only, they invariably forget two small details: First, that they are not their own audiences, but rather somebody else's audiences that they are paying a price for the privilege of interrupting. Second, that they are engaged to whatever they are doing, which rarely translates to engagement with the ads advertisers want to show them.

Technology people, for their part, seem to have trouble understanding that the mere fact that you can technically do something does not mean that it makes sense, or that people will play along. Buying a product directly from a TV show is a perfect example of a solution in search of a problem. In other words: Just because you can, it doesn't mean you should.

Second question: Do you interact with TV ads? I usually head up and go to the bathroom. Why in the world would it be any different online, when I'm actively completing an important task or doing something that really interests me rather than just killing time like in front of the TV set?

Imagine what would happen to TV commercials if marketers were able to count how many people went to the loo during commercials. That's more or less what happened with the web, because the other promise of advertising on the Internet, apart from "interactivity", was that you could track!

No more: "Half of my advertising dollars are wasted, but I don't know which half", like Wanamaker loved to quip. [3]

So, is it working? Do people "interact"? Nope. The average

click rate on banner ads is around 0.1%, or one in a thousand, and less than half as much for the old 468×60 banner ad. [4]

It's pretty crude, but the numbers say that you are much more likely to survive a plane crash than to click on a banner ad. [5] And the off chance of something worthwhile happening after that? Like winning a lottery. Not last because a very significant percentage of clicks come from a small numbers of users [6] who are not exactly the "audience" of your dreams. [7]

More numbers: A staggering 5.3 trillion display ads impressions were delivered in the U.S. in 2012, with Q4 seeing the most at 1.4 trillion – up 6% from 2011. AT&T ranked #1 with 104.8 billion ad impressions. Microsoft came in second with 47.4 billion impressions. No fewer than 445 different advertisers delivered more than a billion banner ads in 2012. [8]

So, what is going on here? Is everything fine, or not really? This is an industry in which more than half the banner ads cannot even be viewed by users [9], and in which a blank banner ad gets more clicks than the average branded one. [10] But for some it works. It's just a matter of price, numbers and number-crunching. Or so they want us to believe. [11]

Compare these billions of banner ads with the following: Apple's "1984" iconic commercial was shown once only, during that year's Super Bowl. Lyndon Johnson beat Barry Goldwater in the 1964 Presidential Elections by showing the famous "Daisy" ad only once. [12] Or consider the impact of the Xerox commercial by George Lois with a chimp making copies of documents. [13] Or that it took only 90 days to Car Ally's counter-attack campaign for Hertz to break Avis and cause them to stop their brilliant and up to then incredibly successful "We Try Harder" campaign. [14]

Not fair, you say? Perhaps not. These are, indeed, some of the best advertising campaigns of all time. But is there a single banner ad campaign you remember? A single banner ad campaign that will make it into the 100 best or most important advertising campaigns of all time? Not counting the banner ads that asked you to punch the monkey in the face, I mean. [15]

The truth is that what some wanted to be like radio in its early days, and others thought would become better than prime-time TV for ads, has actually turned into a very different beast. The *not very interactive* banner ad industry gone bust after the *New Economy* bubble burst has turned into complicated number-crunching exercises that make banner ads work decently enough for large-scale direct response advertisers. [16]

Notes

1. Cox, Jim, *American Radio Networks: A History*, page 123.
2. Isaac Asimov on the future of E-Learning, in 1988.
   https://www.youtube.com/watch?v=FBv3MDSoDfg
3. John Wanamaker was the founder of the famous Department Store that went by his name, the first in Philadelphia, Pennsylvania, and one of the first in the United States.
   http://en.wikipedia.org/wiki/Wanamaker's

   But was Wanamaker right? What did he mean by "wasted"? Was he really talking about advertising, or about direct response? An interesting theory says that in advertising the part that works is exactly the waste. By investing large amounts of money to put their name, their product and their promise in front of large segments of the population, companies assure consumers that they are a serious company, that they stand behind their product and that they are in it for the long run. This doesn't happen anymore once you target

"audiences of one", as is increasingly done in online advertising. Please see: *The waste in advertising is the part that works.*
http://www.researchgate.net/publication/
4733724_The_Waste_in_Advertising_Is_the_Part_That_Works

4. For click-rates around the world, please see a study by Smart Insights.

    http://www.smartinsights.com/internet-advertising/internet-advertising-analytics/display-advertising-clickthrough-rates

5. If you believe what Solve Media says, you are 31 times more likely to win a prize in the Mega Million lottery, 40 times more likely to give birth to twins, 87 times more likely to get accepted to Harvard, 279 times more likely to make your way to Mount Everest, and 475 times more likely to survive a plane crash than to click on a banner ad.
    http://www.businessinsider.com/its-more-likely-you-will-survive-a-plane-crash-or-win-the-lottery-than-click-a-banner-ad-2011-6

6. Interestingly, only 8% of Internet users account for 85% of clicks.
    http://www.comscore.com/Insights/Press-Releases/2009/10/comScore-and-Starcom-USA-Release-Updated-Natural-Born-Clickers-Study-Showing-50-Percent-Drop-in-Number-of-U.S.-Internet-Users-Who-Click-on-Display-Ads

7. And guess what? It's mostly the poor and the uneducated who click.
    http://www.zephoria.org/thoughts/archives/2007/12/03/who_clicks_on_a.html

8. Please read ComScore's *US Digital Future in Focus* 2013 report.
    http://www.comscore.com/FutureinFocus2013

9. A 2012 ComScore study showed that 31% of ads were not in-view, meaning they never had an opportunity to be seen.
    http://www.comscore.com/Insights/Press-Releases/2012/3/comScore-Releases-Full-Results-of-vCE-Charter-Study

    In 2014, Google put the figure on their own network at 56%.
    http://uk.businessinsider.com/google-display-ad-viewability-study-2014-12

10. If you think a click-through rate of 0.04% is an indication of anything, you might just as well divine the future from a goat's innards.
    http://adage.com/article/digital/incredible-click-rate/236233

11. For a good laugh, see Goodby Silverstein & Partners' *Click, Baby, Click!* commercial for Adobe. For a more detailed discussion about online ads and if and how they are working, please see Chapter 9.
    http://goodbysilverstein.com/work/adobe-were-back

12. Twitchell, James B., *Twenty Ads That Shook The World: The Century's Most Groundbreaking Advertising and How It Changed Us All*, pages 184-193 and 154-161.

13. That was exactly 55 years ago. Legend has it that some wise-guy managers placed bananas on their secretaries' desks; following the secretaries' complaint to Xerox, the commercial never aired again.

http://simplifywork.blogs.xerox.com/2015/02/28/first-ever-installation-of-a-xerox-copier

14. Cracknell, Andrew, *The Real Mad Men*, pages 125-131 and 138-143.

15. I don't remember any memorable banner ad. Some people have a better memory than I do. Steve Harrison, for example, rightly says that Amnesty International's "Hangman" banner ad was brilliant. True. But how many times was it seen? Clicked on? Was it talked about at the water cooler at the office or in schools? Did it change the world, or was it merely a good creative execution in a failed ad format? Harrison, Steve, *How To Do Better Creative Work*, Chapter 5.

16. What reputable companies are using online ads for is less clear.

3

Dear Miss Afflerbach

In March 1961, San Francisco advertising maverick Howard Luck Gossage placed an odd ad for Eagle Shirtmakers in *The New Yorker* magazine, which had a circulation of about 400,000 copies. The ad called for people to mail in a coupon to Miss Afflerbach at the company's headquarters in Quakertown, Pennsylvania in order to receive a piece of cloth with a buttonhole and a pocket – a Shirtkerchief, or was it a Shirtkin, or a Napchief? – of dubious use or value. [1]

Something incredible happened: The company received 11,342 coupons. Many people gave a smart answer to the question being asked, i.e. what use was a pocket in a handkerchief/napkin, and a book with the best letters to Miss Afflerbach was eventually published [2], giving yet more visibility to the publicity stunt. Why did it work so well? For one thing, few ads are smart, witty and involving, and so the ones that do stand out have a good chance at striking it big.

Today, in the era of "interactive advertising", 400,000 banner ads would lead not to 11,342 returned coupons, but to 400 clicks if you're lucky, and so at most to 100 people asking for the Shirtkerchief, or less than 1% of the results Gossage was able to bring home for his client. Why? Because banner ads are smaller than ads in *The New Yorker* and don't take up the whole page? Sure. But even when ads on the web occupy the whole screen, results are only marginally better.

Another pertinent answer is something Gossage loved to say: Because advertising sucks and there's just too much of it. [3] Plus, the way an ad is perceived depends not merely on the editorial content, but also on the other ads it shares space with. Ads in *The New Yorker* were not sold to anybody who was ready to pay for them. There were complicated rules, and quotas; a real curation process was in place.

Even though the Editorial Department and the Advertising Department were physically separated, on different floors of the 25 W. 43rd Street building that was home to *The New Yorker*, there was this idea that they should "regard the magazine as a whole". The Advertising Department went out of its way to find new campaigns they liked, and vetoed ads they disliked. Only classy ads they thought their readers would find interesting, tasteful and sophisticated were allowed. [4]

Today, with real-time bidding [5], every single banner ad impression is up for grabs and is assigned in an online auction that lasts a fraction of a second to the advertiser willing to pay the most for it. This is great for direct response, but less for the quality of the ads. Factor in poor creativity, ads that try to fool you to click, dubious advertisers and aggressive retargeting campaigns, and we can well say that if ads in *The New Yorker* were classy, advertising on the web has been everything but. [6]

Last but not least, there is the unspeakable truth in an era in which we have come to idolise social media: *The New Yorker* was much more of a real social network and of a community than Facebook or Twitter ever were or ever will be. *The New Yorker* was "both an extension of the individual and a place of communion to which they came for their shared experience". [7]

Nothing like this can be said with a straight face about either Facebook or Twitter. Why not?

What are Twitter and Facebook? Twitter is a distributed link-sharing system, just like Reddit is a centralised link-sharing system. Facebook is many things: A place where you share jokes and photos of your cat and kids. A way to connect with friends living on the other side of the planet. A feed reader, and more. Facebook is what we used to have before Facebook, i.e. the Open Web, but behind closed doors, delivered very well and a bit sanitised. And we love it, don't we? [8]

But the one thing it's not is a community. Facebook is just a tool: A big forum, even though that doesn't sound very "web2.0". A utility, as Mark Zuckerberg himself likes to say. [9]

By July 1922, less than two years after the first commercial radio station started broadcasting from Pittsburgh [10], "400 volunteer radio stations had sprung up across America". [11]

These words reminded me of RadioPossibility, the hosted blog service started by Marek, a brilliant writer and engineer living in Texas I somehow got to know. Back in 2001, Marek invited me to set up my blog at dotcoma.radiopossibility.com. In those days, we were positively sure that the web would become more and more decentralised. David Weinberger wrote *Small Pieces Loosely Joined*. [12] Chris Locke wrote *Gonzo Marketing*. [13]

One of the big ideas behind those books was that, as people found more interesting things to read on far-flung blogs than they did on lame web portals and on traditional news outlets, it was going to become increasingly difficult for advertisers to chase these readers ("targets", in marketing speak). Not everybody was optimistic about what was going on. Andrew Keen was so worried that he wrote a book saying that blogs written by amateurs were actually destroying our culture. [14]

Little does it matter if you believed we were closer to a new Renaissance or to the end of times. The pendulum has swung the other way. Larger blogs have either morphed into more traditional media companies, or have been acquired by such companies. The *one man band* blog written by an expert in his field or an enthusiast has been all but wiped out by Facebook [15], which web designer and web critic Jason Kottke presciently called "the new AOL" as far back as 2007. [16]

While Facebook is a very successful company, some interesting questions remain unanswered. Is Facebook a force for good in this world? Is it a positive and liberating force? [17]

Is Facebook any good for companies that want to try to interact with their customers? Lastly: What about advertising on

Facebook? Could the fact that we're missing a common shared vision of the world like the one we had as readers of *The New York Times* or of *The New Yorker* be detrimental not only to the fate of our democracies, but to advertising as well?

Notes

1. Harrison, Steve, *Changing the World is the Only Fit Work for a Grown Man*, pages 76-79. For the Shirtkerchief Ad, please see: *http://www.adbuzz.com/OLD/GossageGallery/EagleB.jpg* *http://www.adbuzz.com/OLD/GossageGallery/EagleC.jpg*

2. Gossage, Howard Luck and Harris, Miller, *Dear Miss Afflerbach.*

3. "Is Advertising worth saving? From an economic point of view, I don't think most of it is. From an aesthetic point of view I'm damn sure it's not; it is thoughtless, boring, and there is simply too much of it". - Howard Luck Gossage, as quoted in Gossage, Howard Luck, Goodby, Jeff and Bendinger, Bruce, *The Book of Gossage*, page 4.

4. ibid, pages 133-153.

5. Please see Wikipedia's definition of real-time bidding. *https://en.wikipedia.org/wiki/Real-time_bidding*

6. Even AdWords has a similar quality problem, Google being forced to axe no fewer than 500 million bad ads in 2014. *http://www.theverge.com/2015/2/3/7964671/google-adwords-ebola-scams-fake-vacation-bad-ads*

7. Harrison, Steve, *Changing the World is the Only Fit Work for a Grown Man*, pages 106-7.

8. I actually miss the Open Web, to be honest with you.

9. It's kind of funny when the pundits accuse Mark Zuckerberg's company of turning into what he said it was all along: a utility. *http://techland.time.com/2013/11/17/of-course-facebook-is-a-utility*

10. KDKA is a radio station from Pittsburgh, Pennsylvania that was created by the Westinghouse Electric Corporation in 1920. *http://en.wikipedia.org/wiki/KDKA_(AM)*

11. Twitchell, James B., *Twenty Ads That Shook The World*, page 75.

12. Weinberger, David, *Small Pieces Loosely Joined: A Unified Theory Of The Web.*

13. Locke, Christopher, *Gonzo Marketing: Winning Through Worst Practices.*

14. Little did he know about how bad things would get with Facebook and

Twitter! Keen, Andrew, *The Cult of the Amateur: How blogs, MySpace, YouTube, and the Rest of Today's User-generated Media Are Destroying Our Economy, Our Culture, and Our Values.*

15. This point is controversial. WordPress keeps on telling us that blogging keeps on getting bigger. However, few if any studies on the *blogosphere* have been released after 2011 or 2012 the latest. *http://www.nielsen.com/us/en/insights/news/2012/buzz-in-the-blogosphere-millions-more-bloggers-and-blog-readers.html*

16. Jason Kottke presciently called Facebook "The new AOL" back in 2007. He was right. Facebook is a closed and private Internet. At the same time, one must recognise that they have been profitable for years; that their success has been absolutely incredible, and their execution close to perfect. The way they fended off the attack coming from Google's G+ speaks miles about how good they are. *http://www.kottke.org/07/06/facebook-is-the-new-aol*

17. Some people say that they can read things on Facebook that are not given any attention to in the mainstream media. But with a feed reader, you get to read all the posts of every blog you choose to follow. With Facebook, you see what Facebook thinks you will enjoy. This is what Eli Pariser calls "the filter bubble". They are the ones who hold the remote control, not you. Furthermore, filter bubbles don't merely hide part of the news from us; they also make us live in an "emotional world". Eli Pariser, *The Filter Bubble: How the New Personalized Web Is Changing What We Read and How We Think*, page 150. Not to mention the pseudoscientific *Brave New World* experiments they play on us. *http://www.theatlantic.com/technology/archive/2014/06/everything-we-know-about-facebooks-secret-mood-manipulation-experiment/373648*

4

Social Media Marketing

Strange as it may sound, the notion of social networks comes from academia. In the 1920s, the idea that the modern world was "shrinking" due to the ever-increasing connectedness of human beings became popular. The Hungarian Frigyes Karinthy [1] went a step further and said that any two individuals could be connected through at most five acquaintances – hence the famous *six degrees of separation* – starting from our social network. Unlike The WELL [2], when Friendster, MySpace and later Facebook and Twitter came along, they were all immediately called "social networks".

Two other buzzwords plagued us during those same years and then disappeared. Coined by O'Reilly to launch a conference and the idea that the web was back after the Bubble, "web2.0" is the term used to define a bunch of very diverse websites that had precious little in common except corny names, rounded edges and a tagcloud. [3] Nobody said it better than Sir Tim Berners-Lee: "I think web2.0 is, of course, a piece of jargon, nobody even knows what it means. If web2.0 for you is blogs and wikis, then that is people to people. But that was what the web was supposed to be all along". [4]

Together with web2.0 came the horrible but very telling idea of user-generated content (UGC). According to this crude view of the world, people were using – or being used, and being duped into using, if you listen to Richard Stallman [5] – web-based tools little more than to provide content against which advertisers could place their ads. [6] Then at some point the whole circus started being called "social media". Why the word "media"? Are social media what social networks become once you try to monetise them by sticking ads all over the place? [7]

Account-based Marketing. Affiliate Marketing. Affinity Marketing. Agile Marketing. Algorithmic Marketing. Alliance Marketing. Ambush Marketing. Analytical Marketing. Article Marketing. That's just the A's. Apparently, there are more than 160 types of marketing. [8]

Once you have social media, then of course you have social media marketing. It sounds much nicer than social network marketing or web2.0 marketing, doesn't it? According to Wikipedia, social media marketing is the process of gaining website traffic or attention through social media sites, with efforts aimed at creating content that attracts interest and encourages readers to share it with their friends. [9]

That would make a lot of sense, wouldn't it? [10]

Be interesting! And people will talk about you and spread the word. Oh, if only it were that simple! It is; but apparently there's not a lot of that going on. [11]

Let me tell you what I see a lot of: exactly the opposite. I see a lot of companies sending their customers away from their websites and over to Facebook and Twitter and Instagram etc. Saying "We're on Facebook" or "Follow us on Twitter" must be the dumbest thing of the decade. They're already on your website. Why send them away?

First, because most companies don't like their customers, whom they usually call "consumers", and don't want them bumming around, leaving comments or asking questions on their pixel-perfect websites that smell like death. [12]

Second, because the average company is not very interesting and would thus have a hard time getting involved in social media marketing activities as described above, i.e. in getting their customers to spread the word about them.

Third, because of the hype cycle. They are told there's a "Twitter Revolution" going on in Iran. [13] That Dell is having a huge success selling on Twitter. [14] And that social media were crucial to the success of Zappos. [15] None of this is true, but little does it matter. Everybody agrees that it's a new world, that things will never be the same again, that it's land-grabbing time, and that you need to get in early and make a killing etc. Which is the same nonsense we heard when the pundits were extolling the wonders of the *New Economy*, in case you forgot. Which you probably did.

Lastly, because Facebook made them an offer they could not refuse: There are hundreds of millions of people on our social network, and it's free to contact them. Free marketing! Nothing could be more appealing to the average marketing manager who thinks his company's "messages" are so incredibly important that they belong even in places where people connect with their friends. No need to be interesting: Get, buy or bribe people to "like" your company and then shove your messages down their throats like there's no tomorrow.

So off you go. You create a Facebook Page or a Twitter account for your company, i.e. an official, boring corporate presence in a place where people go to goof off while at the office, connect with friends and relatives, exchange jokes and share pics of their kids or cats. Then you start churning out "content" for people to "consume". Why do you do it? Because it's free!

That's right: You create content for a proprietary platform where you don't own anything, where your posts are readable by members only and don't get indexed by Google, and where it's next to impossible to search [16] what you wrote in the past. Even worse, more often than not you will outsource this task to a web PR agency, which of course means higher costs (so much for free!) and a close to zero chance that your posts will show any personality at all or a human voice.

When you find out, to your great surprise, that people couldn't care less about your efforts, what do you do? Let go of that stiff attitude of yours and try to become more interesting? No, that would be against your corporate policy! You start spending money to attract more people to your Facebook Page on the off chance that they will click on that "like" button and then read the dull posts that the greatest market research tool ever invented – the web – already told you nobody wants. [17]

To sum it up: Instead of attracting people to your website by being interesting to the point that they will want to share your content via social media, you do the opposite. You send your users away from your website to social networks run by other companies where the best you are able to do is to push your boring marketing messages. If they don't travel, you push harder. Instead of relying on word-of-mouth, you shove it down their throats. Best of it all, you call it "conversations". [18]

Notes

1. The Hungarian Frigyes Karinthy was the first proponent of the theory of the *six degrees of separation*.
   http://en.wikipedia.org/wiki/Frigyes_Karinthy

2. When the WELL came around, the catch-all buzzword was "community". As Jacob Nielsen said in 1997, "One of the latest buzzwords to agitate the Web is 'community'. In fact, most Web sites have less sense of community that a New York City subway car". Mendelson, B. J., *Social Media is Bullshit*, page 86.

3. What is web2.0? A brilliant marketing stunt. Please see (in Italian) "Il web2.0: una brillante operazione di marketing". Metitieri, Fabio, *Il Grande Inganno del Web2.0*, pages 19-23.

4. IBM developerWorks interviews Sir Tim Berners-Lee.
   http://www.ibm.com/developerworks/podcast/dwi/cm-int082206txt.html

5. Richard Stallman tells *The Guardian* that cloud computing is a trap.
   http://www.theguardian.com/technology/2008/sep/29/
   cloud.computing.richard.stallman

6. The worst ads ever. "Now with the advent of new media, 'consumer generated content' and 'social networking' it seems there is a conscious effort to dumb down the message to the point you would expect it to be painted in day-glo colors on the walls of your local Toys 'R' US". Parker, George, *The Ubiquitous Persuaders*, page 79.

7. Or, as Gary Vaynerchuk put it when asked that very question: "It's the

Internet. It's the modern word for it. It's the new word. [...] You know what social media is? It's web2.0. You know what web2.0 was? It was the Internet". Mendelson, B. J., *Social Media is Bullshit*, page 16.

8. Here's the complete list. You can't make up shit like this: Account-based Marketing. Affiliate Marketing. Affinity Marketing. Agile Marketing. Agricultural Marketing. Algorithmic Marketing. Alliance Marketing. Ambush Marketing. Analytical Marketing. Article Marketing. B2B Marketing. B2C Marketing. B2P Marketing. Behavioral Marketing. Below-the-line Marketing. Blackhat Marketing. Brand Marketing. Brand Lover Marketing. Brick and Mortar Marketing. Buzz Marketing. Call Center Marketing. Call-to-Action Marketing. Campus Marketing. Catalog Marketing. Cause Marketing. Celebrity Marketing. Channel Marketing. Close Range Marketing. Closed Loop Marketing. Cloud Marketing. Communal Marketing. Community Marketing. Computational Marketing. Consumer-Generated Marketing. Content Marketing. Contextual Marketing. Conversion Content Marketing. Conversion Rate Marketing. Cooperative Marketing. Corporate Marketing. Cross Marketing. Cross-Media Marketing. Data Marketing. Data-Driven Marketing. Database Marketing. Defensive Marketing. Digital Marketing. Direct Marketing. Direct Mail Marketing. Direct Response Marketing. Disruptive Marketing. Diversity Marketing. Door-to-door Marketing. Drip Marketing. Ecommerce Marketing. Email Marketing. Entrepreneurial Marketing. Ethical Marketing. Evangelism Marketing. Event Marketing. Expeditionary Marketing. Facebook Marketing. Field Marketing. Flanking Marketing. Freebie Marketing. Free Sample Marketing. Geomarketing. Global Marketing. Green Marketing. Guerrilla Marketing. Horizontal Marketing. Humanistic Marketing. Inbound Marketing. Industrial Marketing. Influencer Marketing. Informational Marketing. In-game Marketing. In-store Marketing. Integrated Marketing. Interactive Marketing. Internet Marketing. Internal Marketing. International Marketing. Keyword Marketing. Left-brain Marketing. Local Marketing. Long Tail Marketing. Loyalty Marketing. Mass Marketing. Megamarketing. Mobile Marketing. Multichannel Marketing. Multicultural Marketing. Multi-level Marketing. Neuromarketing. New Media Marketing. Newsletter Marketing. Next-Best-Action Marketing. Niche Marketing. Non-traditional Marketing. Offensive Marketing. Offline Marketing. One-to-one Marketing. Online Marketing. Outbound Marketing. Outdoor Marketing. Out-of-home Marketing. Pay-per-click Marketing. Performance Marketing. Permission Marketing. Personalized Marketing. Persuasion Marketing. Point of Sale Marketing. Post Click Marketing. PPC Marketing. PR Marketing. Precision Marketing. Product Marketing. Promotional Marketing. Proximity Marketing. Pull Marketing. Push Marketing. Real-time Marketing. Referral Marketing. Relationship Marketing. Remarketing. Reply Marketing. Reverse Marketing. Scarcity Marketing. Scientific Marketing. Search Marketing. Search Engine Marketing. Seasonal Marketing. Self Marketing. Self-referential Marketing. Services Marketing. Shadow Marketing. Shopper Marketing. Shotgun

Marketing. Social Marketing. Social Media Marketing. Social Pull Marketing. Sports Marketing. Stealth Marketing. Street Marketing. Targeted Marketing. Technical Marketing. Telemarketing. Test-driven Marketing. Time Marketing. Trade Show Marketing. Traditional Marketing. Transactional Marketing. Undercover Marketing. User-generated Marketing. Vertical Marketing. Video Marketing. Viral Marketing. Web Marketing. Word-of-mouth Marketing. Youth Marketing.

9. Please see what Wikipedia has to say about social media marketing.
    http://en.wikipedia.org/wiki/Social_media_marketing

10. It would make a lot of sense. As does trying to track if all this "sharing" brings in results for your company. An interesting solution to help you do that is offered by Lisbon-based startup GetSocial.
    http://getsocial.io

11. According to Wikipedia, successful social media marketing campaigns include the 2008 US Presidential Election campaign; a 2010 petition to have actress Betty White host Saturday Night Live; a short film called "Kony 2012" released by humanitarian group Invisible Children, Inc.; Nike's 2012 "Make It Count" campaign and the San Francisco Bat Kid campaign to help a young boy fighting acute lymphoblastic leukaemia. Is that it? A presidential candidate who captures the hopes of a nation; an actress; one of the largest advertisers ever with one of the coolest products ever and two heart-touching non-profits. How is this supposed to work for those who sell more mundane things like mobile phone plans, margarine and orange juice?
    https://en.wikipedia.org/wiki/Social_media_marketing#Campaigns

12. "The dogs have it right. Customers want to take a good long whiff. But companies so lobotomized that they can't speak in a recognizably human voice build sites that smell like death" - David Weinberger.
    http://cdn.oreillystatic.com/radar/r1/02-00.pdf

13. Foreign Policy magazine on the "Twitter Revolution" in Iran.
    http://foreignpolicy.com/2010/06/08/the-twitter-devolution

14. Dell Says It Has Earned $3 Million From Twitter, *The New York Times* reports. For a company with total revenue of about 60 billion dollars a year, that is about 0,005%. A major hit. For their PR Department.
    http://bits.blogs.nytimes.com/2009/06/12/dell-has-earned-3-million-from-twitter

15. Oh, but Zappos was a huge success thanks to social media, right? Not according to Zappos CEO Tony Hsieh, who said: "Our goal is to build personal, emotional connections with people, whether they are customers, employees, or our vendors/business partners. Twitter (for example) just happens to be one way to do it, but so is the telephone. Nobody cites Zappos as a "telephone success story", so I think it's a bit strange to cite Zappos as a "social media" success story". As quoted in Mendelson, B. J., *Social Media is Bullshit*, page 92.

16. Facebook relaunched Facebook Search in December 2014. Now it's

going to be easier to find that embarrassing post of yours from that night when you drank a beer or three more than you should have.

17. In the worst-case scenario, this means creating false users, which is not merely stupid, but actually hurts your brand because Facebook thinks that they are real people who do not respond to your posts. *http://www.copyblogger.com/bye-facebook/*

18. Tom Fishburne on *The 7 Deadly Sins of Social Media Marketing.* *http://tomfishburne.com/2014/09/socialmedia.html*

5

Butter... You Talking to Me??

The year was 1976, and the guy asking "*You Talking to Me??*" of course was Robert De Niro in *Taxi Driver*. [1] Nowadays, it's to butter and breakfast cereal and shaving foam that want to have "conversations" with me on Facebook and Twitter that I'd ask that question. Conversations with a brand of butter? What happened? Why has this bullshit come to pass as something perfectly normal?

Why is there so much (unwarranted) enthusiasm for social media in the business press? Let me answer with another question: Who creates the narrative about the web in the media? Those who think that the most important thing in life is business and who invariably view the web as just another "media". Which, no doubt about this, means another place where companies should buy advertising.

As a consequence, we were told that the web was doing poorly when things were bad for advertising, like after the Bubble – which was really just a Ponzi scheme in which web portals sold banner ads to new websites whose goal was to sell banner ads to the following round of hopefuls, forever. Or until somebody said enough was enough and the whole thing burst. Once the web was cool again – web2.0, remember? – companies were told they couldn't miss out on the new opportunity to "connect with consumers". But none of this is true.

The web was not doing poorly after the Bubble burst. Blogging was taking off, and so was Open Source software. Google was emerging, and was hiring talent let go by the *dot.coms*. Little more than a decade after the KGB had left the country, Skype was being programmed in Estonia, allowing the world to become a much smaller place. Worldwide, usage of the web kept going up. It was only those who thought they'd sell stupid banner ads at ridiculously high prices or those who wanted to sell dog food online that were doing poorly.

Similarly, when web2.0 and social networks, all of it later dubbed social media, started to emerge, the same people took to praising the success of such websites as if it were proof that the web had finally come of age as an advertising medium. But the two things are largely unrelated. I attended a number of IAB-sponsored events in which the "logic" seemed to be: A lot of people are using blogs and YouTube or MySpace, and later Facebook and Twitter and Whatsapp and what not, so now would you please start buying "display ads" – you know, banner ads, the "interactive ads" nobody "interacts" with – on our web portals and online newspapers?

I sat in disbelief, thinking: Is this really the best they can do? To sum it up: The web is a huge success with end users, no matter how well or poorly online ads sell. Social media: the same. But being a success with the public is different from being a good place for companies to promote themselves.

Unfortunately for companies, Facebook appears to be exactly the kind of place where people goof off and interact much more – to the tune of thousands of "likes" and hundreds of comments every day! – with the same exact photograph of Italian pop singer Toto Cutugno, which is posted every day on a dedicated Facebook Page [2], than they do with the elaborate social media efforts of 99% of brands. [3]

But no, you don't understand. It's different this time around. Consumers want to have "conversations" with companies. Really? Are you serious? I mean, who wouldn't? Call me an introvert, but I don't want to talk with any company that produces butter or yogurt. [4] Call me unromantic if you wish, but I don't want a "relationship" with any company, and certainly not a relationship that is managed by CRM software or by somebody who works for a PR agency.

When was the last time you saw a company or an executive that wanted to have conversations? [5] With whom? With the next person in line at the supermarket to buy soda or beer? The great vast majority of companies have little to say except:

"We're the leaders in..." and "Buy our product". And as the saying goes: If you got nothing to say, then sing it! In other words, are we sure social media are the right place? For mass-market products, I would just stick to TV.

Now, I'm not saying that interaction with consumers is wrong. After all, even soap producers have 1-800 numbers, and apparently somebody calls in sometimes. You should, of course, do the same on Facebook and Twitter. Answer questions and help out your customers who are having problems. In fact, do it right and you have most of what you should be doing on social media covered. [6]

But one thing is to help your customers, and another is to pretend they want to "engage in conversations" with you and then use that lame excuse to feed them marketing messages. This travesty is a complete betrayal of what was said by *The Cluetrain Manifesto*. [7] Online, we talk to one another. The real conversations are between customers who often know more about products than the companies that produce them. If customers of this type want to speak with people who work for a company, it's with the Product guys, not with Marketers, PR flacks or your company's web PR agency.

The Internet could be a great tool to get in contact with and nurture your brand's advocates. The rewards could be huge, but it's certainly not an easy road to travel. [8]

For most companies, it's ok as long as customers ask questions, but what does the average company do if they offer suggestions, or hack their products? Lego could tell you that it's great, but Lego for sure is not the average company. [9]

Most companies are scared to death about getting out of their steel and glass castles and having to open up to the outside world. Look at their uninspiring advertising. Look at their lame websites. But all of a sudden they want to be hip on social media? Who do they think they're kidding?

The *new new thing*, at least at the time of writing, is that social media is important for customer service. But it's funny that companies that excel at customer service don't brag about how cool they are because they do it via social media. [10] How and why should the basic customer service done on Facebook or Twitter be considered an incredible advance? An incredible advance over what? Over doing it the proper way, for example via email and Zendesk? How much does the average corporation spend on CRM software? Is that software integrated with what they're doing on Facebook and Twitter? Do they import the threads, file the data and have access to the people they replied to? If not, is all that software useless? Are posts and replies via social media all they need? [11]

Most important of it all, is it working? Take KLM: Wow, I read they're making 25 million Euros a year from social media. [12] Which works out approximately 0.1% of their revenue. They manage an average response time of 23 minutes, which means that if you ask them a question on Twitter, you might still make your flight. And they reply to you in 11 languages, soon to be expanded to 14. How many people do they employ for this trick? Are they making that incredible 0.1% of their revenue thanks to these "conversations", or rather thanks to advertising on social media? I asked, and nobody answered. Most likely, that revenue is generated by behavioural retargeting, or showing ads to people who had previously visited their website. If this is true, they may be closing the sale, but they are not creating any new demand for their services. Which is what advertising used to be about. [13]

Notes

1. Robert De Niro asking "You talking to me??" in *Taxi Driver*. Thanks to Carlo Andrea Pattacini for the link and for the title of the Chapter. *https://www.youtube.com/watch?v=lQkpes3dgzg*

2. Please take a look at "La stessa foto di Toto Cutugno ogni giorno", or "The same exact picture of Toto Cutugno every day". *https://www.facebook.com/totocutugno666*

   Even *The Washington Post* had something to say about it: *http://www.washingtonpost.com/news/the-intersect/wp/2015/02/06/ the-curious-case-of-the-facebook-page-that-posts-the-same-thing-every-day*

3. Please see what Nigel Rahimpour has to say about the "engagement", or lack thereof, of people on social media with brands. *http://www.psfk.com/2015/02/nigel-rahimpour-marketing-forrester-brand-loyalty.html*

4. Or dishwasher detergent. "The company formerly known as Reckitt Benckiser", now simply RB.com, has signed a nine-figure global deal with Facebook to "move away from advertising". Ah, the irony! *http://www.mediapost.com/publications/article/231386/rb-signs-nine-figure-global-deal-with-facebook-to.html*

5. Conversations? *All I can hear, I me mine, I me mine, I me mine* – The Beatles (George Harrison)

6. It's true, there is of course some know-how involved here. But far less than the web PR agencies of the world would have you believe. Ever noticed that these days nobody talks about "PR crises" anymore? They have been conveniently rebranded "social media crises". Conveniently for whom? For the web PR specialists.

7. Levine, Rick, Locke, Christopher, Searls, Doc and Weinberger, David, *The Cluetrain Manifesto: The End of Business as Usual.*

8. "Why do rock stars have fans and companies have customers? Because that's what both groups want". A very interesting theory from Collier, Mack, *Think Like a Rock Star: How to Create Social Media and Marketing Strategies that Turn Customers into Fans*, pages 3-7.

9. For Lego, see Garfield, Bob, *The Chaos Scenario*, pages 176-183, and

the MIT Sloan Management Review's *Lessons From the Lego Group*.
http://sloanreview.mit.edu/article/collaborating-with-customer-communities-lessons-from-the-lego-group

10. See Zappos. Or Nordstrom. Garfield, Bob, *The Chaos Scenario*, page 73.

11. Relation Desk is a Swedish startup that sells a smart solution to handle your customer service on social media. Nice. But I ask: Does it offer any integration with your company's CRM software?
http://www.relationdesk.com

12. KLM: "We make €25m per year from social media". But they won't tell us how. To paraphrase what Churchill famously said about Russia, social media is a riddle wrapped in a mystery inside an enigma.
https://econsultancy.com/blog/65752-klm-we-make-25m-per-year-from-social-media

13. Retargeting serves ads to the 98% of people who visited an E-commerce website but left without buying. Which is a good way to try to close the sale, but not to create or increase demand for a product or service. Which is what advertising used to be about.
https://en.wikipedia.org/wiki/Behavioral_retargeting

6

Lies, Damned Lies, and ROI

I am nothing less than fascinated by how social media has caught on with large companies. Small businesses, I get it – managing a Facebook presence is much easier than creating a website. Point taken: If you're a bakery or a coffee shop, forgo the website, open a Facebook Page, speak from your heart, tell your story and give it a try, by all means.

But for large companies, it's different. Your company has a website, and it should use it. Read the definition from Wikipedia again: The goal should be to create interesting things on your website that people will want to spread. [1] Blog posts, white papers, info-graphics – even ads, if they're good, and not to send people over to Facebook or Twitter where you bore them with content nobody would ever think of sharing.

Plus: you are in charge of your website. I hate to break it to you, but you don't own Facebook. [2] That's their website. They are the ones who can and will change the rules to further their interests, not yours. Social networks should be a tool to help your customers and your fans – your fans in the real world – share the good news about you to their friends, i.e. potentially to a much larger audience than you will ever be able to reach, and not yet another outlet where you can do more talking. [3]

So, let's say your company is doing it all wrong. You shut down your blog; keep your corporate website nice and clean, i.e. dead; send your customers over to Facebook and Twitter and Pinterest and Tumblr and Vine and Vimeo and Instagram and to any other shiny new thing that pops ups, and then invariably force-feed your followers the same staid corporate messages (yes, "conversations").

Why in the world, you ask? Beats me. But more importantly: How do you justify this strategy?

How does your company decide whether its social media efforts are successful or not? Do you set goals? Because if not, then anything goes. [4] After the initial enthusiasm, it's now full of people busy covering their tracks and suddenly talking about "The ROI of social media marketing".

Let's take a closer look. Some go to great lengths to explain basic things such as how much it costs to acquire a "like". Which is fine. But what good is a "like", or a follower on

Twitter? How do they influence the bottom line? A "like" is the equivalent of getting somebody to sign-up for your newsletter – except that it's Facebook that is going to be sending your updates, and only when and if they fancy. It's similar to getting somebody to opt-in to receive your paper catalogue at home, if you still send one out. Does that lead to people buying your products? Because if it doesn't, then what's the point of it?

Others cite "research" that highlights that those who are fans of a brand on Facebook tend to spend more with that brand than those who are not. No surprise here, right? Only, this correlation does not demonstrate that this happens because I am a fan. I saw ads of a product, or a friend told me it was a good product, so I bought it. Then perhaps I "like" it on Facebook. Not the other way around. [5] Sorry, but if you spend money to get people to "like" you thinking that you're "automagically" creating a customer who is worth x dollars to your company, you must be on low-quality drugs. [6]

Some agencies are trying to convince you that the right thing to do is to compare your page views on social media to advertising impressions, the idea being to prove that it's cheaper to distribute your marketing message on social media than it is to buy ads on somebody else's content. [7]

There's a social media agency in Milan, Italy that is adding up the number of impressions from a client's Facebook Page, Twitter account, YouTube presence etc, or apples and oranges and pears, and then arbitrarily calls the sum "reach". [8]

An advertising agency in Zagreb, Croatia is trying to calculate the value of a Facebook Fan by (over) estimating the number of "impressions" the average poor fellow would tolerate receiving on the part of a company before calling it quits. [9]

Too bad that in theory your social media presence should not be advertising – remember all the hoopla about those "conversations"? And, in any case: Even if it were advertising, the goal of advertising is not just to secure ad space on the cheap, but to deliver results. The mere fact that it may be cheaper to deliver a message on social media is not enough. The correct question you should ask is: "Are we getting more or less of a bang out of the money we are spending on it?". [10]

In other words, a certain number of "likes", a certain number of impressions, or "a good sentiment", i.e. a subgroup of your customers having a positive image of you, are, at best, intermediate goals. What about real results?

Has any company managed to increase market share or profits thanks to social media? Or, at the very least, has any company managed to increase the number of people who ask for information about their products or who google them? [11]

A few years ago, Kia Motors launched a campaign on Facebook for the Kia Soul, a so-called "urban passenger vehicle". The campaign was a success because it built a "brand community" of 89,000 people – or a nice Facebook Page where people could chit-chat, in case you're wondering what that means. As a result, we learn that "the brand can reach over 31 million friends of those fans with Friends of Connections Targeting". [12] That's right: Thanks to this campaign, Kia can now pay Facebook to reach more people with more (paid) ads. Apparently, that's how you measure success these days.

Oh, yes, and there was a 13% increase in awareness for the Kia Soul, according to a study conducted by media research firm *The Nielsen Company*, and 14% of individuals who said their perception of the Kia brand improved. Sounds good. But do those percentages refer to the whole of the American population, or to those 89,000 fans? It doesn't say. Which means they are talking about 13% of those 89,000 fans. Almost regardless of how much money was invested in this campaign, is improving what 12,000 people think of you worth the time and effort, if you're a mass-market company? [13]

Notes

1. Media companies companies that have been successful with their Facebook strategy all kept their own websites and use Facebook to push people to their websites, not the other way around.

2. You don't own Facebook and you're not in control. See Camisani Calzolari, Marco, *Escape from Facebook*.

3. All this is so wrong and so stupid. It seems to misunderstand the fundamental change we have witnessed: That on the web – not just on social media – everybody can talk.
   http://www.dotcoma.it/2010/03/28/your-companys-urge-to-tweet.html

4. If you don't set clear goals, whoever took your marketing budget is going to make up a brilliant success story ex-post for you about how many fans or tweets, retweets or something similar you got. He or she is almost certainly going to give you a beautiful colour report as well. Enjoy it, put on a nice face and hope your boss will like it, too!

5. Thanks to Bob Hoffman for pointing to this hilarious piece of "research" produced by Syncapse! Hoffman, Bob, *101 Contrarian Ideas About Advertising*, pages 112-114.
   http://www.syncapse.com/value-of-a-facebook-fan-2013

6. Low-quality *New Economy* drugs, to be precise. Remember when all the *dot.coms* were saying that every subscriber to their newsletter was worth hundreds of dollars? You don't? See, that's the problem.

7. This is just plain wrong. I never liked the new trilogy of "owned media", "earned media" and "paid media". Every time people gave me that jingle, I rolled my eyes over. But if we want to use it, we should use it correctly. Owned media means a company's website,

their Facebook presence, Twitter account and other social media channels, their catalogue, leaflets and so on. What we used to call "collateral". Earned media is the free "publicity" a company can get when people talk about them, either in the traditional media or in blogs, social media etc. Not the "free impressions" they get on social media, even though that's exactly the way many companies seem to "understand" and use social media. Paid media, of course, is advertising. Goldgeier, Dan, *Killer Executions and Scrubbed Decks: An Outside-the-Box Look at Obnoxious Advertising and Marketing Jargon*.

8. Here are the numbers for a campaign TheGoodOnes did for Sony, and the random sum they arbitrarily call "reach".
http://thegoodones.eu/blog/i-numeri-della-campagna-playsony

9. Degordian, an advertising agency based in Zagreb, Croatia, tries to calculate the value of a Facebook Fan.
https://www.facebook.com/notes/degordian/what-is-true-value-of-your-1-facebook-fan-answer-is-2646/295241268427

10. The fact that producing content may be cheaper than buying ads is simply not enough. What are you getting out of it?
http://www.adotas.com/2014/05/surviving-the-adpocalypse-what-will-you-do-when-the-current-model-stops-working

11. The more a campaign's "success" is judged by "likes" or "engagement", the smaller an effect it has on the bottom line. What happens in Vegas stays in Vegas. I am very sceptic every time one of these social media websites tries to convince companies to spend marketing money to achieve what I call "internal results", i.e. results about how they position themselves on their platform instead of real-world results. Likes, fans, followers, tweets, retweets, impressions. All fine. But what about sales? "Do you want to see the goddam sales curve stop moving down and start moving up?", as Rosser Reeves used to say. Please see Reeves, Rosser, *Reality in Advertising*.

12. Please read the results of the Kia Soul Facebook campaign on Scribd.
http://www.scribd.com/doc/97390210/Kia-Facebook-Ad-Case-Study

13. B.J. Mendelson goes on to say that even if all the fans who said they had more awareness of the Kia Soul ended up buying the car, which of course is absurd, that would still count for less than 0.7% of Kia's revenues. And the figure is more likely to be somewhere closer to 0.007%. Mendelson, B.J., *Social Media is Bullshit*, pages 105-6.

7

The Real Value of a Facebook Fan

I feel your pain. I can almost hear you: I'm having fun reading this little book of yours. But it's time to get down to business. I want to know what the real value of a Facebook Fan is. Only, I know nothing about your business. How am I supposed to tell you? And the same, trust me, is true of most of the social media consultants who line up to pocket your money.

Ok, let me try. Your boss wants you to get "likes" at $4 a pop? That could be the real value for you. Unless, of course, you want to try to sit down with him or her and work out a better idea, like trying to think what your company could use these "likes" for, apart from getting an ego boost.

If you're the one in charge, it's harder. You have to decide for yourself what you want to get out of your marketing money. All I can tell you is: Beware of "experts". Why? For example, because experts seem to have a hard time agreeing what the real value of a Facebook Fan is.

$214.81 for non-profits, according to a 2012 study by Blackbaud, NTEN, and Common Knowledge linked by Business Insider, but currently unavailable. [1] Please note the decimals: A clear sign that we're dealing with professionals here, not dumb people like you and I.

$136.38 according to Syncapse, when Business Insider tried to shed a light on the subject in 2012, but apparently as much as $174 in 2013. [2] A 28% percent increase, as they love to boast. Me, I'd love to ask them if sales for their clients have increased as much from 2012 to 2013!

$26.46 according to Degordian, an advertising agency in Zagreb, Croatia that is trying to (over)estimate the value of a Facebook Fan based on the number of posts from a company that a poor fellow will tolerate receiving before deciding to "unlike" the company. [3]

About $10, "assuming a constant cost-per-click of $1", as I read on AdAge. [4] Does that mean that the more money I squander to acquire a fan, the more he or she will end up being worth to my company? An interesting theory if there ever was one. And probably a wrong one, too. If I "bribe" a person to "like" my company in exchange for a discount, for example, he or she is likely to be worth less to my company, not more.

$8.00 according to ChompOn, a white-label flash-sales group-buying third-party plug-in solution. Oh, I'm sorry. I'm having a little fun with the language marketers love to use. But the figure is interesting, given that flash-sales websites tend to be high-value businesses that convert well.

$3.60 according to Vitrue [5], which calculates the value more or less in the same way Degordian does but comes to a much lower number. But one still too high for charities to buy. [6]

$1.34 in ticket sales, according to Eventbrite. The idea of seeing who of your friends goes to an event doesn't work well. In the real world, nobody wants to show up uninvited.

$0.21 in sales, according to Ecwid.com, the second largest store-building application on Facebook. This means 1/40th of what a fan is worth according to ChompOn (see above).

$0.00 or exactly zero, according to Forrester Research [7], which states the obvious: It's what companies do with fans that creates value, not merely having fans. Ask not what your fans can do for you, but what you can do for your fans. Getting people to sign up for your updates on Facebook, because that is what getting a "like" means, does not mean that you have the right to send them marketing messages until the cows come home. Or until they "unlike" you.

-$100.00 (with a minus sign). Perhaps a fan is worth -$100, in the case of Pepsi. That is, $100 to their red-and-white competitors based in Atlanta, according to Bob Hoffman. [8]

In 2010, Pepsi decided to sit out of the Super Bowl for the first time in over 20 years and invested in a social media project named *Pepsi Refresh* instead. The campaign called for individuals and organisations around the US to submit to the *Pepsi Refresh* website ideas that could transform their communities for the better, and for people to cast their votes for the best ones using either their Facebook account or an account they created on purpose on Pepsi's website.

The *Pepsi Refresh* project was a success in many ways: PepsiCo funded 676 ideas with a total of $21,350,000 in grant money. [9] The campaign increased Facebook "likes" by more than 600 percent, to 3.5 million, and generated more than 140,000 tweets. The RefreshEverything.com website brought in no fewer than 17 million unique visitors and a total of 4.5 million votes were cast for the best ideas. [10]

Unfortunately, sales of the sugary drink and of its "diet" counterpart Diet Pepsi were down 5%. Sales for Coke and Diet Coke stayed flat in the same period, and Diet Coke overtook Pepsi as the second best-selling soft drink in America. The drop in sales for the Pepsi brand was worth about $350 million. Divide that number by 3.5 million "likes" on Facebook, and at long last we have the figure we were looking for. Each "like" was worth $100. To *The Coca-Cola Company*. [11]

Notes

1. Nice job, Business Insider! I added a few more estimates to their list. The study by npENGAGE is offline at the time of writing. *http://www.businessinsider.com/what-is-a-facebook-like-actually-worth-in-dollars-2013-3*
2. Not only Syncapse have trouble understanding the difference between

correlation and causation; in the *Lucy in the Sky with Diamonds* world they live in, BMW's Facebook Fans are valued $1,613 each.
http://www.syncapse.com/value-facebook-fan-consumer-brands-174

3. For what it's worth, I disagree with both the reasoning of advertising agency Degordian and with the figures they give.
http://www.dotcoma.it/2014/10/29/the-true-value-of-a-facebook-fan.html

4. According to social media agency SocialCode, as reported in AdAge.
http://adage.com/article/digital/study-facebook-fan-worth-10-average-brands/231128

5. Social media specialists Virtue, now part of Oracle Social Relationship Management, put the value at $3.60.
http://www.adweek.com/news/technology/value-fan-social-media-360-102063

6. Charities are known to be among the best at evaluating the return on their investment. Not surprisingly, they are not too impressed even with those who say that Facebook Fans are worth $3.60 apiece.
http://www.futurefundraisingnow.com/future-fundraising/2010/05/whats-the-value-of-a-bogus-study-of-facebook-fans.html

7. This blog post from Augie Ray at Forrester Research is worth reading.

   http://blogs.forrester.com/augie_ray/10-07-08-what_value_facebook_fan_zero

8. Anybody who is speaking out against the folly of "social media marketing" owes a lot to the Ad Contrarian, American adman Bob Hoffman. His *101 Contrarian Ideas About Advertising* is a must-read.

9. Please take a look at this case study put together by Emily Kamischke, a Master's student at Elon University.
http://www.studymode.com/essays/Project-1830572.html

10. More info on *Pepsi Refresh* can be found on Stephanie Perry's blog.
http://sites.psu.edu/sperry5483/2014/03/24/pepsi-refresh-project-case-study

11. Brilliant. Please see Hoffman, Bob, *101 Contrarian Ideas About Advertising*, pages 183-5 and 201.

8

Quod Erat Demonstrandum

There were many signs that the hysteria was out of control. The *Land O' Lakes* logo that asked consumers to connect with their favourite butter on Facebook is probably a spoof from a social media consultant. [1] But the company does have a Facebook Page, where they share recipes with their "fans" and get blasted for feeding GMO corn to their cows.

Two other cases scream of "jumping the shark" moments. First, *Banco do Brasil* changed their home banking interface to "make it more social". [2] What was the idea, to share one's transactions with one's friends and make possible messages like: "Hey Mark, why haven't you paid me? I happened to see that you received the money transfer from Kate". [3]

The second comes from Europe: at the height of the love affair with Facebook, the Czech Republic's Tourism Board decided to rebrand their country, which had been known to the world for a mere twenty years under that name, to *Czech RepubLIKE*. [4] What was wrong with the Czech Republic? [5] What did they achieve with this ridiculous *dot.com era* trick? [6]

Amid this absurd excitement about anything "social", with companies racing to set up a Facebook Page to pump their marketing messages to their fans for free, Facebook had to step in. On the one hand, they needed to protect their users from companies' voracious appetite for free marketing in the form of way too many posts. On the other, they could profit.

In 2012, Facebook told companies that what they started calling "organic reach" [7], by which they meant the percentage of a company's fans who would receive that company's oh-so-important marketing messages, was being limited to only 16% of their fans on average. Time Magazine said it was only 6%. [8] There is little doubt that it will slide further. [9]

What this means is very simple: The free lunch is over. The real value of a Facebook Fan is close to zero. Want to reach more of your fans? Pay. And guess what? The lower the organic reach, the better Facebook's stock price started to look. [10]

What about the other social networks? The trend towards paid visibility is either happening or will happen soon on Twitter, Instagram, Pinterest and even SoundCloud. [11]

It's just part of the script. Take Instagram, for example.

At first, they gave away free visibility. To build a few successful case studies and entice the big names, they invited over companies that produced products like skateboards or "fixie" bicycles. As companies that produced ketchup and dishwasher detergent were having trouble being as cool, Instagram sold ads to them so that they could build up their follower base.

Sure as anything, our timelines are soon going to be choking full of photos of "cool" Ford Mondeos and of 26 different flavours of Brand-A jam. That's when Instagram will cut back on organic reach, just like Facebook did, and start charging companies if they want to reach a larger percentage of their followers. And who am I to blame them? It's a brilliant strategy. Only, I ask: Why do companies take the bait? [12]

Does your company want to buy ads on Instagram? Just like Twitter and Pinterest, Instagram too is going to give you access to "analytics" and beautiful colour reports about your impressions, reach, frequency, likes, retweets and re-pins. Everything except anything even remotely related to sales. [13]

Are these stats worth the pixels they are displayed on? Probably not. So why do people obsess over them? For the same reason I have always been a big fan of Alexa. Not accurate? Perhaps not, but who cares? Their stats are free, web-based, simple to use and come with nice coloured graphs!

Beware any time the metrics are focused on a platform's internal usage. Especially if there's no volume and if it's just a pet project to make your company look smart. How many times are the photos of your products seen? The more, the merrier! But does that help you sell more stuff? If it doesn't, you're wasting your time, money and focus.

So what happens now? A friend who works for a large Italian company told me that only a couple of weeks after they found out that only a small percentage of their fans were seeing their updates due to the new algorithm, responsibility for the company's Facebook Page was passed from Marketing to PR.

At Kraft, they see things differently. Julie Fleischer, *Director of Data, Content and Media,* said the obvious but yet unspoken and very welcome truth: Brands shouldn't post content they don't deem worthy of paying to distribute. Content marketing makes sense only if the content you produce is good enough that you want to pay to distribute it. [14]

Pay to give visibility to your posts, or just buy ads. That's right. This is what this hyper-hyped social media thing will boil down to: ads. Ads against user-generated bullshit (UGB). Which is fine, because there's nothing wrong with ads. It's how newspapers and radio stations and TV channels pay the bills and turn a profit. But enough with "conversations".

Show ads to people when they Google products in your category, bring them over to your website and then, if they don't buy, retarget them on Facebook. [15] Looks like the perfect one-two punch to me. But please stop calling it a "revolution". It's just user-generated chit-chat. And loud-mouthed guys coming on air and shouting: "How white my shirt can be". [16]

Endless times, it seems.

Notes

1. "No, I don't want to be friends with my butter. Brand Relationships in the Social Media Era", a presentation by Nathaniel Perez. *http://www.slideshare.net/mahumbaba/no-i-dont-want-to-be-friends-with-my-butter-brand-relationships-in-the-social-media-era*

2. Please see: *Banco do Brasil Transforma Internet Banking em Orkut.* *http://tecnocracia.com.br/banco-do-brasil-virou-orkut*

3. My 2 cents' worth on banks that want to be "social". *http://www.dotcoma.it/2012/08/19/your-bank-wants-to-be-social.html*

4. The *Czech RepubLIKE*. So brilliant that they wanted all the world to know about it. In as many languages as possible. *http://www.23hq.com/dotcoma/photo/20572520/original* *http://www.23hq.com/dotcoma/photo/20572523/original*

5. What was wrong with the Czech Republic? Things that pop to mind when I think of the Czech Republic are great beer, thermal baths, the Velvet Revolution and Václav Havel. What's wrong with any of that?

6. What did they achieve with this ridiculous *dot.com* era trick? Not much. It's all gone, even their *Czech RepubLIKE* Facebook Page. *http://www.23hq.com/dotcoma/photo/20572524/original*

7. The Facebook post about lower organic reach, 23 April, 2012. *https://www.facebook.com/marketing/posts/10150839503836337*

8. Citing research from Ogilvy&Mather, Time magazine disagreed and reported that organic reach was only 6%. *http://time.com/34025/the-free-marketing-gravy-train-is-over-on-facebook*

9. Valleywag: Facebook to slash organic reach to 1 or 2 percent. *http://valleywag.gawker.com/facebook-is-about-to-make-everyone-pay-1547309811*

10. A chart explaining why Reachpocalypse is great for Facebook. *http://www.convinceandconvert.com/social-media-tools/this-chart-explains-the-reachpocalypse-and-why-facebook-is-laughing-all-the-way-to-the-bank*

11. Build a large enough mousetrap, and then splatter ads all over it. Now it's SoundCloud's turn. Do we ever stop for a second and wonder what this tells us about our culture and our societies? Gossage did. *http://www.nytimes.com/2014/08/21/business/media/popular-and-free-soundcloud-is-now-ready-for-ads.html*

12. Even more shocking to me: Why are companies apparently happy to be schooled on how to do an effective campaign on these platforms by twenty-somethings who may know every possible trick about Instagram and Twitter and Pinterest, but who have never spent a penny in their lives trying to sell products?

13. You can measure almost everything that doesn't matter with the

"analytics" tools from Twitter at analytics.twitter.com, from Pinterest at analytics.pinterest.com and of course from Instagram, too! *http://blog.business.instagram.com/post/95314562151/businesstools*

14. "If you wouldn't spend money behind it, then why do it? It's shouting into the wind without making a sound". Thanks, Julie. *http://adage.com/article/best-practices/kraft-content-drive-broader-marketing-effort/294892*

15. And on mobile, too. You know, cross-platform, multi-device, that kind of mumbo jumbo. And, much more importantly, big, in-your-face formats, not the small ones nobody notices on Facebook's website.

16. *(I Can't Get No) Satisfaction*, by The Rolling Stones

9

———

What Would Gossage Do?

What would Howard Luck Gossage do – and what would he not do – were he around today? Why Gossage?

First, because he tried and was successful at many things we would call "interactive" and "social" today. For example, he did not plan a whole campaign, but preferred to write one ad at a time, in order to gauge how the public reacted before writing a second ad. This, rather than clicking (hardly ever) on banner ads, is what he liked to call "interactive". [1]

Second, because "Every profession bears the responsibility to understand the circumstances that enable its existence", as sociologist and architect Robert Gutman said. [2]

Very few people in advertising ever cared half as much as

Gossage about trying to think deep and hard about the business they were in, and very few left a body of writing so interesting and so critical of advertising. [3]

What was Gossage good at? Crafting for his clients stories that were full of wit and humor – stories that travelled well with customers and the press alike. He experimented in ways we can compare to social media in times when such tools were not available and companies did all the talking.

What did he despise? The endless repetition of a message just because it "kind of worked". Advertising is "a seventeen-billion-dollar sledgehammer to drive a thirty-nine-cent thumbtack", he said. [4] A large part of what follows is about what Gossage would not do. I think it makes sense, given how sceptic he was about advertising.

Gossage was a self-proclaimed generalist, honest in not wanting to offer too many services to too many clients and good at keeping his ad agency nimble and focused. [5] Were he around today, he would keep his client list short, say no to clients he disliked and to clients he thought he could not help or for whom he did not recommend any advertising at all. [6]

Gossage would understand that today your product, your website and the way you treat your customers and your workforce define who you are as a company much more than your advertising or the cheesy tricks you try to play on social media. He would probably be the only one in advertising happy about the lessened role of advertising.

Gossage was a master at creating ideas that would make people send back coupons, but he would insist your company find somebody with the technical skills to drive traffic to your site via SEO and SEM because, in spite of all the bullshit we are fed on a daily basis about the importance of social media, those are still and by far the two most important traffic channels. [7]

What about advertising on the web? Gossage would not buy banner ads for any of his clients, and he would insist that they don't via anybody specialised in the field, either.

Gossage would be appalled by what is happening online. He believed that buying ads was a privilege, not a right, and that newspapers and magazines belonged to the readers, not to advertisers. On the web, we have become accustomed to "news" websites that are created to attract traffic thanks to SEO and to make money with Google AdSense.

While advertising on the web truly looks like "shooting fish in a barrel" and the game is rendered more scientific by the day, the fish are not only "not holding still as well as they used to", as Gossage said. [8] They are actively arming themselves to get rid of ads. In 2014, 41% of Americans under the age of 30 used an ad-blocking tool to surf the web without ads. [9]

Even more important: Banner ads are unable to change the perception the public has about a brand.

Do you disagree? Please tell me about a banner ad campaign that had an effect similar to the "We Try Harder" campaign. Creativity is not very important in online advertising, and that's one of the reasons why the big conglomerates where you wouldn't find an ounce of creativity if you looked all day love to push it: It's a pure media and number-crunching play where creativity doesn't matter. [10]

Do you think Gossage would be crazy not to take advantage of the hyper-targeting and segmenting opportunities offered by online ads? Maybe so, but he's not alone. Smart companies are starting to understand that it's not worth the hassle to buy banner ads and risk being associated with low-level publishers or with the many low-level advertisers they would be sharing space with even on serious websites. While Microsoft bought 47 billion banner ads in the US in 2012, Apple is backing off. Apple had a European affiliate marketing program with TradeDoubler in the early 2000s. It's gone. [11] Apparently, they understood that it's not a good idea to pay websites to display their banner ads alongside advertisers such as casinos, dating websites or ringtones. Or Microsoft, for that matter. [12]

Lastly, I'm sure Gossage wouldn't buy banner ads because there is very little proof they work. Sure, the tracking systems tell us that a user "has seen" a certain banner ad, and will speculate that even though he did not bother to click on it, he was in fact influenced by it when, on a later date, he searched for something on Google and then converted.

But can we trust this to be true, especially when Google is selling not only AdWords on the search results, but also a large part of those banner ads via DoubleClick? Another good question is: Is this educated guess made on ads that users have really seen, or on those merely served to them? [13]

And a further one is: Why do we give part of the merit to banner ads nobody clicked on, but fail to do the same with print, radio or TV ads? Or with the fact that merchandise is shown in stores? Or with the strength of some of these brand names? Are banner ads getting a free ride?

Notes

1. See Harrison, Steve, *Changing the World is the Only Fit Work for a Grown Man*, pages 58 and 63. Do you think this is not a big deal? It's huge: it means that you're not trying to impose your point of view, but that you're open to inputs from your readers; it means that you're fooling around, and you know it. Compare this with what Unilever is doing on social media: they create, or at least used to create, when "distribution" was free, at least 360 posts a day on Facebook for their various brands. Creativity and social sharing? Really? It seems more like the Military-industrial complex at work to me.
   http://read.percolate.com/percolate_unilever_case_study.pdf

2. Robert Gutnam, a sociologist, studied the field of architecture.
   https://www.princeton.edu/pr/pwb/07/1210/gutman

3. It is very rare for people in advertising to indulge in talking about the nature and the limits of the business they are in: Not just the technicalities (the "hows") but also the "reasons why". Apart from Howard Luck Gossage, two notable exceptions are George Lois, a very prolific writer and the author of the wonderful: *What's the Big Idea?*, and Jerry Della Femina, who expressed his dissatisfaction with people in the higher hierarchies in ad agencies: "They never talk about advertising. That's a funny thing. These cats talk about advertising only at creative review board meetings". Della Femina, Jerry, *From Those Wonderful Folks Who Gave You Pearl Harbor*, page 105.

4. "Another thing that is likely to breed a certain amount of disrespect for advertising among its practitioners is the triviality that constitutes most of big advertising – a multibillion dollar hammer hitting a thirty-nine cent thumbtack". Gossage, Howard Luck, Advertising and the Facts of Life, in *The Book of Gossage*, page 16.

5. Gossage never employed more than a dozen people at The Firehouse, home to his San Francisco ad agency.

6. See Harrison, Steve, *Changing the World is the Only Fit Work for a Grown Man*, page 38, for how Gossage quit his largest account, Paul Masson Wines, and pages 41-42 for how he told Volkswagen they did not need his services because the Beetle was so good the car would sell itself. The account went to DDB, and the rest is history. For more on the Think Small campaign, see Imseng, Dominik, *Think Small. The story of the World's Greatest Ad.*

7. Social media gets 4 times the coverage of SEO in Techcrunch, and 58 times the coverage in Mashable. But how important is it as a referral source for E-Commerce? 2% of visits to E-Commerce sites are thanks to social media, vs. 34%, or 17 times as much, for SEO. *http://searchenginewatch.com/sew/opinion/2257044/can-we-please-stop-hyping-social-as-the-marketing-messiah*

8. While advertising may indeed seem like shooting fish in a barrel, "there is some evidence that the fish don't hold still as well as they used to and they are developing armor plate". Gossage, Howard Luck, *The Book of Gossage*, page 29.

9. Online, you have reach. More reach with Google Display Network or Yahoo! or Facebook than with almost any TV show save the Super Bowl. And you have targeting. What you don't have is people willing to put up with your ads. In 2014 in the US 41% of people under the age of 30 used an ad-blocking tool of some kind to block out ads. *http://downloads.pagefair.com/reports/adblocking_goes_mainstream_2014_report.pdf*

10. Take French conglomerate *Publicis Groupe*. In January, 2015, after deluding themselves with the idea of merging "as equals" with the much larger Omnicom and then toying around with the idea of a deal with retargeting company Criteo, Publicis acquired Boston-based Sapient. Time will tell if this was a good idea or not, but the press release is pretty clear about the goal of the deal: To have more than 50% of the total revenues coming from the digital space. *http://newsflash.publicisgroupe.net/uploadedDocs/20150206_2015-02-05_Sapient-Closing_FINAL-EN.pdf*

    MoreAboutAdvertising reports that Levy wants his legacy to be to have transformed *Publicis Groupe* into an "Internet" company. *http://www.moreaboutadvertising.com/2015/02/whats-next-for-publlcis-as-it-seals-sapient-deal*

11. Apple currently runs an in-house affiliate marketing program that is a different beast. Not banner ads to promote their iconic hardware products that need little extra promotion, but a set of tools, which include text links, widgets, banner ads and product feeds, to help their affiliates sell *long tail* products such as apps, books and music. *https://www.apple.com/itunes/affiliates*

12. Other companies continue with banner ads, truth be told. The most successful example I know of, at least in Italy, is ING Direct. But even though they are a bank, ING Direct is itself a startup: Worldwide, they had only 300,000 customers in 1999, and reached 23 million in 2010. They have long been the largest advertiser on the web in Italy and have used banner ads very well to close the sale. However, my feeling is that they have built a brand because of their good service (no surprise here) and in spite of their banner ads, rather than thanks to having annoyed millions of people countless times with them.

13. Are we making this guess based on ads that users could at least have

seen, or are we counting the unviewable ones as well? This is an interesting question, given that in December, 2014, Google reported that 56% of the ads served on their network could not be seen! But it's probably another question you're not supposed to ask.
http://uk.businessinsider.com/google-display-ad-viewability-study-2014-12

10

Make Lemonade

What if the web and social media were a lemon not just for newspapers, record labels or travel agencies, but also for advertising? [1] That's right: not interactive advertising. Nor the new frontier of hyper-targeted ads that keep on getting more targeted but fail to really get any better.

What if it were a totally different kind of place where for the first time ever common people got to do as much talking as companies? Where the tone of the discussion has changed forever. Where knowledgeable people speak their minds and companies are often forced on the defensive.

What if, for reasons that are beyond me, I were to "like" my favourite brands of toilet paper, soda, hamburgers, butter, breakfast cereal and shaving foam. Would it be reasonable to think that I wanted to have "conversations" with these brands? Conversations about what, exactly?

Research indicates that only 15% of the people who "like" a brand say it's ok to market to them. Only 0.5% of them interact. Even for aspirational brands such as Harley-Davidson, Ford Mustang, Louis Vuitton, Chanel and Jack Daniels, the interaction is lower that 1%. [2]

On the other hand, many of these erstwhile docile consumers are going to call bullshit on you if you lie to them or try to make nice on the web to cover up dirty practices. What many promised would be a marketer's dream looks more like a nightmare for most companies. [3]

So why do companies love social media in spite of it all?

Because it's the *new new thing*. Because it's hip, sexy and easy. I think companies love social media for the same reason Bob Garfield says they love focus groups: "Because they are cheap"(...); and because: "They make you feel sooooo good. You can sit there on the client side of the two-way mirror and delude yourself into thinking you're getting in touch with the consumer, or the electorate or whomever". [4]

Perhaps fooling around on social media is not easy, but it's easier than having a great product and doing great advertising, of which we see little lately. It's certainly easier than doing business in an ethical way. Companies love social media because, courtesy of the hype surrounding everything "social" and thanks to beautiful coloured graphs and "metrics" that mean very little, it's very easy to fool oneself into believing that everything is ok. [5]

This said, is it not possible to promote one's products on social media? Sure, everything is possible. Or, as Gossage used to say: "People read what interests them, and sometimes it's an ad".

But it's not enough to merely "be on social media" – or, worse, look like fools by comically trying to be on every single new social thing under the Sun. [6] You need to be interesting! Just like on the web. Just like with advertising. You don't "get" the web? The problem, as David Ogilvy famously said, is that you take your customers for stupid. [7]

Social media is the one place in the digital arena where a great copywriter and a great performance artist like Gossage, who did things we would call "social" back in the '60s, would have excelled. So, what should we do? How can we try to make lemonade out of this lemon called the web?

Mack Collier makes it sound a little bit too simple: Be a rock star! [8] Great advice, except: What if you're not? What if your company were more of a boy-band? You know, a marketing play that is out there mostly to make money, but which is confronted by critics, not ecstatic teenage fans.

Write stories, not ads or marketing messages! Better still: Write stories that are not necessarily about the company or the product, like Gossage did. Recognise that the whole thing is a *pièce* of *Théâtre de l'Absurde*. You know, people speaking with brands that produce butter, that kind of stuff.

Especially if you're not Patagonia [9] – which you probably are not, just like 99% of the companies in the world are not – use creativity, humor, wit and grace. Make sure your customers understand you're fooling around. Let them in on the gag. Make them feel part of a community! [10]

Even though he operated in print [11], and in *The New Yorker* any time he could, Howard Luck Gossage's body of work follows along these lines: think about his wacky ideas and wonderful stunts for Qantas, Scientific American magazine, Pink Air for Fina and Eagle Shirtmakers. [12]

Or think about how he engaged – and I mean engaged for real, not just to the tune of a simple "like" from behind a screen! – a whole generation of forward-thinking Americans to do something to change the world, be it to save the Grand Canyon [13] or to stop the war in Vietnam. [14]

So, what to do? Mock companies that are taking it all too seriously? Spoof your company's own "war rooms", monthly meetings and coloured graphs that show how "successful" your social media presence is? If it were successful, you wouldn't need to prove it to anybody, right?

If it were successful, my guess is that "social analytics" would be less important. Your CEO and your Marketing Manager would fool around on your Facebook Page from time to time. Ideally, they'd screw up once in a while, over-promise a customer and get the company sued.

Then you could turn that into a story for the "real" media, i.e. the newspapers and TV channels where you often hear about something cutesy that happened on social media: "CEO tries to do customer care, over-promises and gets sued by irate customer". What a great story that would make!

So, if we do something crazy like this, will it be a smashing success? Will "earned media", which we used to call "publicity" and which is free as in *free speech*, not as in *free beer*, replace costly TV ads? No, probably not. First, because there's no need to "replace" TV. At least according to Nielsen, TV viewing is declining but not plummeting, contrary to what the social media gurus of the world love to tell you. [15] Not to mention: when done right, TV commercials are, unlike banner ads or social media marketing, a proven way to create or increase demand for a product. Second, because social media have much less influence than we are told, especially if they it cannot count on the help of offline media. [16] That's right, that's what success on social media really means: finding a way to get featured in newspapers and on TV for free!

Howard Luck Gossage was great at this. Sadly, those who are convincing companies to invest in social media seem to be better at spinning social media – and their own careers – than at putting social media to use for their clients.

Notes

1. Not merely in the sense of "turning analog dollars into digital pennies", as Jeff Zucker said, but in the sense that it's a totally different world, one in which what companies have to say gets drowned out by the more interesting things we talk about with one another. And a world in which trying to push one's message or acting hip on social media will only make things worse. One of my favourite cases of a company trying to exploit the dynamics of the web and

social media comes from Kellogg's, which is giving away free spoons with one's name engraved on them and is asking people to share their "selfies with their spoons" on social media.
https://spoon.kelloggs.com

A selfie with a spoon? Wow. How do you call this? Chris Locke of Cluetrain fame spoke of MTDs, or *Marketing Transmitted Delusions*.
http://www.rageboy.com/codeblue.html

2. 15 percent said that folks can market to us; 46 percent said it depends on the context and 39 percent said never. Furthermore, only 0.51 percent of "Likers" actually posted any brand-related content of any kind, including so much as a single comment. Even so-called high-interest brands, such as Harley-Davidson, Ford Mustang, Louis Vuitton, Chanel and Jack Daniels all registered below 1 percent. Garfield and Levy, *Can't Buy Me Like*, pages 118-119.

3. Pepsi's *Refresh Project*, apart from not helping them sell more sugary water, was blasted, their efforts accused of being similar to the phony corporate social (ir)responsibility campaigns of tobacco companies.
http://healthland.time.com/2012/06/22/study-soda-companies-corporate-social-responsibility-campaigns-are-harming-your-health/

United Airlines and the hit song *United Breaks Guitars*.
https://www.youtube.com/watch?v=5YGc4zOqozo

McDonald's #McDStories, the hashtag Forbes called a *bashtag*.
http://www.forbes.com/sites/kashmirhill/2012/01/24/mcdstories-when-a-hashtag-becomes-a-bashtag

4. Please see Garfield, Bob, *The Chaos Scenario*, page 196.

5. As I wrote back in 2010: In the meantime, beneath the friendly "web2.0" pose, life goes on as usual at Big Corp. PR flacks push hard to sell their story to newspapers, and perhaps put on hold ad spending if the paper does not comply; negative blog posts are more often than not dealt with by lawyers; and nobody inside the company gets to do any talking except those who have long forgotten how to speak in a human voice. But you have a tag-cloud on your website, and a few thousand fans on Facebook, and followers on Twitter. Life is good, and there's no need to change. No need to change Big Corp's company culture; no need to confront the market; no need to be open and down to earth and accessible; no need to fearlessly show on your website what is being said about you online on blogs and Twitter and no need to let your employees take part in the conversation; no need to be interesting and friendly so that thousands of people will happily spread the good news about you to thousands of their real friends and followers. With a nice "web2.0" mask on you can fool yourself that there's no need (for now) to face up to the fact that Obama, not Eisenhower, is now President and we're not in 1950 anymore.
http://www.dotcoma.it/2010/03/28/your-companys-urge-to-tweet.html

6. McLuhan would have loved this: The only real message is the fact that you use social media. Many companies seem to have taken this too literally, in the misplaced hope that it would be enough to be hip. But there is nothing wrong with ads, if they are smart. And there is nothing inherently good about social media just because it's social media. Especially not if what you use it for is dumb or exploitative. *http://www.psfk.com/2011/12/confessions-of-a-mad-man-gossage-did-it-already.html*

7. "The consumer is not an idiot. She is your wife." - David Ogilvy. Another great adman who understands that people have a knack for good ads and who hates the patronising attitude of many advertising agencies is George Lois: "Too much advertising is predicated on the snobbish assumption that people are dumb, so why give them smart advertising?". Lois, George, *What's the Big Idea?*, pages 59-62.

8. See Collier, Mack, *Think Like a Rock Star: How to Create Social Media and Marketing Strategies that Turn Customers into Fans*.

9. Patagonia's mission is real, unlike many other companies': Build the best product, cause no unnecessary harm, use business to inspire and implement solutions to the environmental crisis. Bogusky and Winsor, *Baked In: Creating Products and Businesses That Market Themselves*, pages 51-2. Patagonia is certainly not your average company: they have even run ads that said "Don't buy this jacket" (unless you really need it, of course).

10. According to Professor Pabst, that "community of interest" can be seen in all those people who drove around with Fina's pink valve cap fitted to their car; followed John F. Stahl's walk to Seattle; wore their Beethoven Sweatshirts or, being avid Mozart fans, formed their own sub-community, "The Wolfgang Club"; the thousands who wrote in to Eagle Shirts with their suggestions on a use for the shirtkerchief; and the amateur aerospace engineers who entered wholeheartedly into the madness of the paper airplane competition. All of them, clipping the coupons and playing their part, were finding togetherness and a shared sensibility. Harrison, Steve, *Changing the World is the Only Fit Work for a Grown Man*, pages 105-6.

11. Gossage never did TV commercials, only print ads plus some radio ads together with comedian Stan Freberg.
http://en.wikipedia.org/wiki/Stan_Freberg

12. For Qantas, see Harrison, Steve, *Changing the World is the Only Fit Work for a Grown Man*, pages 16-19; for Scientific American magazine, see Gossage, Mander and Dippel, *The Great International Paper Airplane Book*; for Fina, see "The Shape of an Idea and How to Draw One", in *The Book of Gossage*, pages 44-58; for Eagle Shirtmakers, see Gossage, Howard Luck and Harris, Miller, *Dear Miss Afflerbach*.

13. Now Only You Can Save Grand Canyon From Being Flooded... For Profit. See Harrison, Steve, *Changing the World is the Only Fit Work for a Grown Man*, pages 114-118.

14. Why I am going to: 1) Wear a black tie; 2) Drive with my lights on in broad daylight; & 3) Keep it up until this war is stopped. See "Two More Rules Gone to Hell", *The Book of Gossage*, pages 184-197.

15. See for example Slide 6 of Nielsen's 2014 The Total Audience Report. *http://ir.nielsen.com/files/doc_presentations/2014/The-Total-Audience-Report.pdf*

    Other studies report a higher decline over time, but not a collapse, and no change at all among the (moneyed) over-50 crowd. *http://www.marketingcharts.com/television/are-young-people-watching-less-tv-24817*

16. How do I know? Look at how books about the social media "revolution" are promoted. Not with Twitter or a Facebook Page, but by reaching out to journalists in the mainstream media.

Afterword

Fairfax Cone said: "Advertising is what you do when you can't go see somebody. That's all it is".

When I learned that Oreo cookies had 18 people on their social media team and only 65,000 followers on Twitter [1], I had one of those "Houston, we have a problem" moments. So, every person on Oreo's social media team caters to only 3,611 followers? Might as well go see them.

During the 2013 Super Bowl, however, Oreo's social media team was quick to react to a blackout at the stadium in New Orleans. When they tweeted: "Power out? No problem" [2] with a link to an ad for Oreo cookies that said "You can still dunk in the dark", apparently they made history.

Really? Is this the "Lemon" or the "You're some tomato" or the "If you're driving down the road and you see a Fina station and it's on your side so you don't have to make a U-turn through traffic and there aren't six cars waiting and you need gas or something please stop in" [3] of the Digital Age?

Mark Ritson, Associate Professor of Marketing at Melbourne

Business School isn't impressed. According to his calculations, even once you count the retweets less than 0.2% of the number of Americans who actually buy Oreo cookies every year saw the ad. How can that impact sales? [4]

Nobody knows.

And companies never learn. [5]

Notes

1. Please tune in to minute 5'15" of Mark Ritson's presentation, *Social Media is the Greatest Act of Overselling in the History of Marketing*. *https://www.bandt.com.au/marketing/social-media-waste-time-marketers*

2. Here's the link to Oreo's tweet that changed the history of... No, it's a good idea. But it didn't change anything. *https://twitter.com/oreo/status/298246571718483968*

3. An analysis of the Volkswagen Beetle's *Lemon* ad. *http://www.writingfordesigners.com/?p=1731*

   George Lois's brilliant campaign for *Wolfschmidt's Vodka*. *http://www.georgelois.com/pages/milestones/mile.wolfschmidt.html*

   Howard Luck Gossage's wonderful *If you're driving down the road* ad. *http://www.adbuzz.com/OLD/GossageGallery/pink4motto.jpg*

4. The only real, demonstrable impact it had was in the business press, which was awash with articles about how Oreo (supposedly) won the Super Bowl ad frenzy, and at the Advertising Awards.

   How Oreo Won the Marketing Super Bowl. *http://www.wired.com/2013/02/oreo-twitter-super-bowl*

   You can still dunk in the dark: awards. *http://www.360i.com/work/oreo-super-bowl*

5. Two years after Oreo, it was *The Coca-Cola Company*'s turn to try their hand at being smarter than the rest on Twitter. For the 2015 Super Bowl, they encouraged Twitter users to mark – or spam, can we say? – negative tweets from their friends with the #MakeItHappy hashtag. Those tweets would then "automagically" be turned into cute art images using ASCII lettering code. Which was kind of nice, until

Gawker created a @MeinCoke Twitter bot that tweeted lines of *Mein Kampf* at Coca-Cola. And so, *The Coca-Cola Company* finally got the attention in the press they wanted so badly: *Tricked Into Quoting Hitler, Coca-Cola Suspends Automated Tweet Campaign.*
http://www.adweek.com/news/advertising-branding/coca-cola-suspends-makeithappy-social-campaign-162775

Acknowledgements

Thanks to all the teachers who have encouraged me to learn, to ask questions and to write. Thanks to Professoressa Pergolo. Special thanks to Professor John Anderson, who was my guide and my supervisor for my thesis at the *Università degli Studi di Milano*, and to Professor Lidia De Michelis.

Thanks to *The Martin Agency* in Richmond, Virginia, for giving me the chance to do an internship in advertising in the Summer of 1998. Thanks to Reinhold Gabloner for having the guts to hire me at ciao|com on the grounds of precious little experience and an extravagant cover letter in 2000.

Thanks to Marek J, who invited me to start blogging on a hosted version of Userland he set up at RadioPossibility.com. Thanks to Gianluca Neri and Nando Nasi for all the help with Movable Type and later WordPress. Many thanks to Andrea Margiovanni for revamping my blog in August, 2014.

Thanks to Steve Harrison for his very well researched and beautifully written *Changing the World is the Only Fit Work for a Grown Man*. Thanks, Steve, for reading an early version of this book, for your precious advice and for insisting that I take a look at the work and words by George Parker.

Thanks to Lucio Bragagnolo, Andrea Andreutti, Walter Vannini, Michele Kettmajer, Francesco Armando, Gaspar Torriero, Simone Brunozzi, Matteo Cassese and Eike Post for reading my manuscript and offering suggestions. Thanks to Roberto Grassilli for the beautiful artwork for the cover.

Thanks to my mother and father for the support, no matter how sceptic they may have been at times about this whole project. Lastly, thanks to the many colleagues, friends and readers of my blog with whom I've had many interesting conversations about the web, advertising and social media.

About the Author

The author of these pages likes to think of himself as a web and advertising expert, accidentally dispersed in one of the fashion capitals of the world. Based in Milan, Italy, he has managed to work in Marketing and Business Development roles for startups from Germany, France, Italy, Sweden and Denmark, before moving to Barcelona to work for yet another startup.

He is currently applying his talents, or lack thereof, towards saving the world by improving how we move around in cities, working for Montreal-based public transport app Transit.

He'd love to hear from you (surname at gmail.com), and he'd really appreciate a review of this work, either at Goodreads or on the website where you purchased this book. Thank you!

www.ingramcontent.com/pod-product-compliance
Lightning Source LLC
Chambersburg PA
CBHW071245020426
42333CB00015B/1628